FROM CATHLEEN TO ANOREXIA
The Breakdown of Irelands

by

Edna Longley

EDNA LONGLEY is a Reader in English at Queen's University Belfast and well-known as a critic of poetry and as a cultural critic. Author of two books, *Poetry in the Wars* (1986) and *Louis MacNeice: A Study* (1988), she is also an editor of the *Irish Review* and on the editorial board of *Fortnight*. ***From Cathleen to Anorexia*** is partly based on her controversial *Irish Times* articles which appeared in Summer 1989.

First published in 1990 by
Attic Press,
44 East Essex Street,
Dublin 2.

British Library Cataloguing in Publication Data
Longley, Edna
From Cathleen to anorexia
1. Ireland. Nationalism
I. Title II. Series
320.5409415

ISBN 0-946211-99-X

Cover Design: Paula Nolan
Typesetting: Attic Press
Printing: Elo Press

FROM CATHLEEN TO ANOREXIA

The Breakdown of Irelands

Northern Ireland has been called a 'failed political entity'. I think it's time to admit that both parts of Ireland are failed *conceptual* entities. That is, the ideas which created them and the ideologies which sustained them have withered at the root. If 'Northern Ireland' has visibly broken down, the 'Republic' as once conceived has invisibly broken down. And since 1968 each has helped to expose the inner contradictions of the other.

In his poem *Aisling*, written near the time of the hunger strike, Paul Muldoon asks whether Ireland should be symbolised, not by a radiant and abundant goddess, but by the disease anorexia:

> Was she Aurora or the goddess Flora,
> Artemidora or Venus bright,
> Or Anorexia, who left
> A lemon stain on my flannel sheet?

In blaming the hunger-strikers' emaciation on their idealised cause, the poem equates that cause with a form of physical and psychic breakdown. 'Anorexia' is thus Cathleen Ni Houlihan in a terminal condition. Anorexic patients pursue an unreal self- image - in practice, a death-wish. Similarly, the Nationalist dream may have declined into a destructive neurosis.

Feminists question any exploitation of the female body for symbolic or abstract purposes. So perhaps Anorexia should, rather, personify Irish women themselves: starved and repressed by patriarchies like Unionism, Catholicism, Protestantism, Nationalism. But here we come up against a difficulty. Not all Irish women resist these patriarchies. And for some, mainly from the North, Cathleen flourishes abundantly still. The Northern women's movement has been divided and retarded; while the Southern movement, preoccupied with church-and-state, has largely avoided 'nation'. Eavan Boland's feminist poem *Mise Eire* (I am Ireland) destabilises Mise but not Eire. There is some reluctance, partly for fear of further division, to re-open the ever-problematic, ever-central issue of 'Nationalism and Feminism'. Later I will ask whether they are compatible. For the moment, I offer the reluctance as symptomatic.

This pamphlet will mainly focus on the ideological breakdown of Nationalism because its breakdown is more complex and less obvious. Nationalism and Unionism are not in fact the same kind of ideology, nor do they function in the same manner. So they differ in their modes of collapse as in their modes of construction. Unionism since the first Home Rule bill has always been reactive: a coalition of sects, interests, loyalties and incoherent hatreds in the face of a perceived common emergency. No totalising philosophy covers the whole coalition, even if religious and secular alarm fuse on its fundamentalist wing. Orangeism and Paisleyism maintain a select tribal memory-bank of historical persecutions, in which emblematic events (1641, 1690) are reinforced by biblical parallels. But this has never developed into a comprehensive symbolic system. You can't personify Unionism. 'Orange Lil' is not the whole story.

As a separatist movement, Nationalism had to put together a more elaborate ideological package and make more absolute claims. Also, like Polish Nationalism, it is informed by Catholic theological habits. When the SDLP and Sinn Féin deny any sectarian component in their politics, these very habits blind them to the seamless join between Catholicism and Nationalism, a join which is a matter of form as much as content. Nationalism thinks of Unionism as heresy - hence past failures to analyse or understand it. And to come up against the church on *ne temere* or integrated education is to be as chillingly excluded as when one meets the guardians of the Republican grail.

Lapsed Nationalists are, therefore, more liable than lapsed Unionists to suffer from metaphysical *angst*. One example is Richard Kearney's compulsion to redefine the platonic Republic. Other Southern writers and intellectuals strangely complain that 'Ireland does not exist'. This seems less an empirical judgement than a state of unconscious mourning for a god, a goddess, a symbolic future that failed. Two other post-Nationalist reactions are revisionism and cynicism. But there has to be *some* reaction. Nationalism was internalised as God, Nature and Family. So it can leave painful withdrawal symptoms as it recedes.

Unionism does not linger like bog-mist in unsuspected crannies. For better or worse, you generally know it's there. Unionism exposes its contradictions in public: in the gap between its interior monologues and what it can get the rest of the world to believe. All ideologies work through unconscious assumptions as well as conscious creeds. But the Unionist unconscious, in both its secular and religious versions, has never been open to outsiders, whereas the reflexes of the Nationalist unconscious have been widely accepted as norms. The situation in the North is not helped by the tendency of Nationalist Ireland to swallow or re-import its own dated propaganda. Patrick Kavanagh once said (with regard to the popularity of *The Quiet Man* in Dublin): 'the only place now where phoney ould Oireland is tolerated is in Ireland itself'. Unfortunately, he underestimated an export-market which continues to boom. When flattered by Irish-American sentiment or left-wing 'Brit guilt', Nationalism becomes less disposed to self-criticism and forgets its inner malaise.

Literature plays a part in all this too. (We import some starry-eyed lit crit from the USA). Now and then I will use contemporary writing as an index of the double ideological breakdown in Ireland.

There are good historical reasons why Irish Nationalism so often reads like bad poetry and Ulster Unionism like bad prose. Cathleen of course has been Muse as well as goddess. Eoin NacNeill tried to lower the political temperature before the Rising by sending round a circular which plainly stated: 'What we call our country is not a poetical abstraction .... There is no such person as Cathleen Ni Houlihan .... who is calling upon us to serve her.' Ulster Protestantism, which prides itself on plain statement, has been slow to evolve a self-critical prose tradition, let alone qualifying clauses. Thus from the 1920s most writers had no option but to constitute themselves an *opposition* to the ideological clamps holding both Irish entities together. In my lifetime, these clamps have distorted ethics, politics, social and personal relations, the lives of women, education, what passes here for religion, and our whole understanding of Irish culture.

Literature remains the primary place where language changes, where anorexic categories are exposed. This is no less the case in Ireland than in Eastern Europe.

IRISH, IRISHER, IRISHEST

'Irishness' is the most inclusive category for Irish Nationalist ideology – and also the most insidious. In the last paragraph of *Modern Ireland* Roy Foster criticises the recurring theme of 'being "more" or "less" Irish than one's neighbours; Irishness as a scale or spectrum rather than a simple national or residential qualification; at worst, Irishness as a matter of aggressively displayed credentials'. Last Easter, Cardinal O'Fiaich proved how this theme persists in the collective unconscious. 'Many Protestants', he said, 'love Ireland as devoutly as *any* Catholic does' (my italics). He then recited the litany of Patriot Prods (Tone, Emmet etc) usually produced in support of such statements. It sometimes seems as if Protestants have to die for Ireland before being allowed to live here.

The Cardinal meant his remarks kindly. But in so deliberately including Protestants, he excluded them. He fed the belief that Protestants have to work their passage to Irishness. Catholics, on the other hand, are born loving the country, knowing by instinct its entire history and literature, and generally 'kinned by hieroglyphic peat' (Seamus Heaney). This nonsense, out of date in the Republic, is widely swallowed by both sides in the North. But Ulster Irishness, like Ulster Britishness, is a state neither of nature nor of grace. It is enforced and reinforced by socialisation, often by simplifications and stereotypes. In *Ripley Bogle* Robert McLiam Wilson satirises the conditioning processes of the North:

> I learnt a great many things on my first day at school. I

> discovered that I lived in Belfast and that Belfast lived in Ireland and that this combination meant that I was Irish. The grim young bint we were loaded with was very fervent on this point. She stressed with some vigour that no matter what anyone else were to call us, our names would always be Irish...[she] told us that the occasional Misguided Soul would try to call us British but that of all things to call us - this was the wrongest. No matter how the Misguided Souls cajoled, insisted or pleaded, our names would remain Irish to the core, whatever that meant... in the spirit of compromise (ever with me even then), I dubbed myself 'Ripley Irish British Bogle'.

Roy Foster would replace the competing indoctrinations with 'a more relaxed and inclusive definition of Irishness, and a less constricted view of Irish history'. Who would not agree? Yet when he developed this idea in his lecture 'Varieties of Irishness', the Unionist David Trimble felt political pressures in the very term 'Irishness', however far its elastic might stretch. Of course Unionists can be equally paranoid about being called Irish and not being called Irish (as Jews in pre-war Poland resented the alternatives of assimilation and expulsion). But this seeming paradox is in fact an accurate response to the rhetorical tactics famously admitted by Senator Michael Hayes in 1939: 'We have had a habit, when it suited a particular case, of saying they were Irish, and when it did not suit a particular case of saying they were British'.

One way of circumventing an elaborate quadrille, in which the dancers contrive never to meet on the same ground, might be to accelerate the separation between political Irishness and culture in Ireland. Culture in Ireland is a range of practices, expressions, traditions, by no means homogeneously spread nor purely confined to the island. Political Irishness, on the another hand, is the ideology of identity ('Irish to the core') mainly packaged by the Gaelic League, which, twined with Catholicism, served to bind the new state. In the Republic the strings of this package have got looser and looser, and much of its substance has leaked out. In the North, Sinn Féin still tries to deliver a fossilised and belated version. There, whether embraced or resisted, Irishness endures as an absolute abstract noun. When threatened by that absolute, Unionists reach for the security-blanket of Britain or Ulster. Meanwhile, they are happy enough with relative or adjectival usages: Northern Irish, Irish Protestant, even Irish Unionist. In these usages, Ireland stands for the country, not the nation, and 'Erin's Orange lily' feels at home. The often-put question 'Are you British or Irish?' is strictly meaningless, since 'Irish' does double duty as an allegiance and as an ethno-cultural description. 'British' is only an allegiance, an umbrella for English, Scots, Welsh and some Northern Irish. Allegiance has cultural effects, and culture influences allegiance. Yet 'Britishness' is not *opposite* to 'Irishness': it is the affiliation whereby Ulster Protestants seek to maintain those aspects of their identity which are threatened by political Irishness.

Perhaps their reactions might seem less paranoid after we have visited the political unconscious of Alban Maginness, SDLP Councillor in Belfast. Here he is replying to an article by John Wilson Foster in which Foster contends that 'Northern Protestants have been excluded by the Nationalist majority in Ireland from being Irish'. Maginness says:

> Curiously, in some non-political situations, the Northern Protestant, which Foster unapologetically claims to be, concedes, asserts or even claims Irishness ... the train loads of rugby supporters from Belfast to Lansdowne Road ... bear witness to [it]. A tired and over-worked example some might say, but it does raise the question, why can't this 'sporting' patriotism be translated into political patriotism? My understanding of modern Irish history is that the majority culture was and still is inclusive, not exclusive and has an almost missionary zeal to persuade if not cajole Northern Protestants into realising or owning up to their innate Irishness ... why this absurd denial of Irishness? (*Studies*, Winter, 1988)

The above manifests a deep confusion between cultural and political Irishness. Maginness's rugby example should indeed be laid to rest since the only group *not* heading for Lansdowne Road are Ulster Catholics. The culture of sport is heavily politicised in the North, keeping talent from the great games of rugby and hurling. And surely Maginness answers his own questions when he finds Irish Protestants, Irish Unionists relaxed about their affiliations to this country - a different matter from patriotic acceptance of the Republic - when the political heat is turned off. (People constantly generalise about 'Ireland' when they mean the Republic.)

Maginness might also compare his own feelings whenever Unionism proposes to 'include' him, or professes 'missionary zeal' about persuading him to own up to his innate Britishness. And what exactly should Foster be *apologising* for?

As Unionists shy away from cultural areas that seem appropriated by Nationalists, so Nationalists assume that cultural 'Irishness', very narrowly defined, functions as a prelude to the political variety. A *cúpla focal* on the lips, a twiddle on the fiddle, and 'from their full and genial hearts/ An Irish feeling [will] burst.' Labhrás O Murchú actually told the New Ireland Forum that 'any Unionist who is exposed to the *Tobar an Duchais* will come up with a much more legitimate status for himself than the status that was contrived'. (This is the same man who decided that traditional Irish music opposed abortion.) The celebrated dulcimer-player John Rea was an Orangeman who, although always friendly toward Catholic fellow-musicians, called them 'Them' to the end of his days. False hopes and fears are invested in 'the convert syndrome'. This encompasses the Protestant Gaeilgeoir as well as the Protestant patriot. Unfortunately, all converts impress the congregation they join a lot more than the one they have left. (They may also be subtly patronised as heretics who have seen the light.) A type of Aran-knit Ulster Protestant is particularly misleading in this respect, and has no battalions at his (or her) back. But even if East Belfast were teeming with potential Douglas Hydes, it doesn't follow that the language leads to the nation. After all, Samuel Ferguson set out to show that Gaelic literature is not the exclusive property of Catholics and Nationalists. Mutterings to this effect have even been heard from the vicinity of the UDA.

What about literature in English written by Irish people? Does it belong to the nation, the country, the island, these islands, the world? Patrick Kavanagh knew he was on dangerous ground when he claimed that 'the writers of Ireland [are] no longer Corkery and O'Connor and the others but Auden and George Barker':

> Saying this is liable to make one the worst in the world, for a national literature, being based on a convention, not born of the unpredictable individual and his problems, is a vulnerable racket and is protected by fierce wild men.

John Banville has been able to say more coolly that 'there is no such thing as an Irish national literature, only Irish writers engaged in the practice of writing'. Yet when progressive cultural thinkers in the Republic dwell on the Europeanism or Atlanticism of Irish writing, they sometimes forget that its Irishness has been shelved rather than interrogated. For naive readers some Irish writers and texts are still more Irish than others. And, thanks to the Irish Literary Revival, the canon retains a vaguely Nationalist aura, abroad if not always at home.

This is ironical, given that some literary critics have problems with Yeats's English literary connections, and with his latter-day cult of the Anglo-Irish Ascendancy. But if Yeats's Protestant and English affiliations were more sympathetically regarded, it might illuminate the role of the North in Ireland's literary culture. Still quoted is AE's dictum: 'Unionism in Ireland has produced no literature'. This, like Irishness and Britishness, involves a false alternative whereby anything written by Irish people can be turned to the glory of Nationalism. Meanwhile, Protestant cultural expression is caricatured as drums and banners (not that the interest of these should be overlooked). Such perceptions reproduce an image foisted by political Irishness on to political Protestantism (and sometimes internalised by it). This image excludes the dual Irish-British context, and what Protestants actually write, paint and perform, whatever their political allegiances.

In 1985 Gerald Dawe and I edited a collection of critical essays entitled *Across a Roaring Hill: The Protestant Imagination in Modern Ireland*. To some, the category appeared sectarian (whereas 'Irish' would have been taken for granted). One reviewer (Declan Kiberd) assumed that we had a hidden Unionist agenda; another (Enoch Powell) assumed that we belonged to the Nationalist conspiracy. Brendan Kennelly quoted an acquaintance who reacted to the book's title by declaring that 'Protestants have no imagination at all'. This stereotype partly results from the inhibition of artistic expression within Scottish and Ulster Calvinism. But instead of putting down that culture with reference to 'the wonderfully rich Irish literary tradition etc' it should be understood in its own terms. Again, the relation of all Irish writing to Protestantism and Catholicism, an issue masked by homogenising 'Irishness', should be opened up - as should relations between Irish and English literature after 1922.

So I think that 'Irishness' with its totalitarian tinge, ought to be abandoned rather than made more inclusive. To include/exclude the Ulster Prods involves another false alternative (cf Senator Hayes) with underlying Nationalist assumptions. 1798 is no more practical use to us than 1916. Charles Haughey may have pragmatically modified his views since he made his opening speech to the Forum. Yet, in his psychic alarm, he identified the real agenda: 'The belief has been canvassed that we would have to jettison almost the entire ethos on which the independence movement was built and that Irish identity has to be sacrificed to facilitate the achievement of Irish unity.' In fact, some such sacrifice may be necessary for the sake of peace let alone unity as once dreamed. But cultural change and changing awareness of culture, in the Republic and even in the North, have already exposed political Irishness (the 'ethos on which the independence movement was built') as now more a prison than a liberation.

NORTHERN NATIONALISTS AND SOUTHERN REVISIONISTS

When Nationalism achieves its object it 'begins to die'. So said Sean O'Faolain in 1951. This means that the relation between Southern and Northern Nationalism is one of uneven development. The

Southern state was gradually born into evolution, while Northern Nationalism (like Unionism) froze in an archaic posture. It stayed bent on realising what Revisionism now seems wantonly to discard. But perhaps Northern Nationalists, nearly as anachronistic in Dublin as the Unionists in London, will have to accept that the Southern clock cannot be stopped or wound back.

As Clare O'Halloran shows in *Partition and the Limits of Irish Nationalism,* between Northern and Southern Nationalists there lies a distance not only of time but experience, a distance usually disguised by rhetorical togetherness. She quotes John A Costello on the adversarial imperative that gives Northern Nationalism its distinctive shape: 'they have to fight their fight up there as a minority, and every piece of Protestant bitterness in the North has its counterpart, both politically and in a religious sense, in the hearts and in the actions of a Northern Catholic. We in the South have got to recognise that we cannot understand that problem or appreciate it to the full.' That applies whether you are shocked by the atavisms of the North, or whether you don't want the North to rock the (relatively) secure Southern boat.

The affair of Conor Cruise O'Brien, Garret FitzGerald, Senator John A Murphy and the SDLP was a tremor produced by the largely unexamined relation between Northern and Southern Nationalist consciousness. This relation rarely reaches the political surface, because there is assumed to be not relation but identity: identity of perception, interest, objective, context, historical moment. In this case tensions surfaced over SDLP attitudes to the RUC. Yet the emotional temperature of the row, particularly the reflex to execrate O'Brien and protect Hume, soared above its occasion. That signalled psychic alarm: the alarm-bells that ring whenever Northern Nationalism and Southern Revisionism touch.

In fact to deny any split or breakdown within the Irish Nationalist psyche is to deny well-attested trauma. The South's long neglect of Northern Nationalists (documented by O'Halloran) breeds guilty over-compensation - which does not necessarily heal underlying resentments. (Go back, Austin Currie.) But Senator Murphy's hostilities, like O'Brien's certitudes, may be unwise in trying to break a taboo with a crowbar. Meanwhile slagging the South goes down well in West Belfast, and opinion in the Republic swings between indifference and feverish identification. The latter, however, is mostly roused by events which concern 'British justice' (the Gibraltar killings) and thus recall shared experience before 1922. In my view such philosophical and political incoherence serves neither side in the North, and retards the Republic's maturation into being part of the solution rather than central to the problem. It might advance the Hillsborough Accord if psychic separation were promoted not only between Britain and the Unionists, but also between the Irish Government and Northern Nationalists.

Even *Irish Times* editorials can regress towards political infancy when championing the SDLP: 'the SDLP and Provisionals may share, in part, a mistily defined political objective - the unification of Ireland. That is not an illegitimate objective: indeed it is a noble and attractive ideal' (22 April 1989). The last twenty years have seen the nemesis of misty definitions and attractive ideals. As for 'noble' (an adjective generally reserved for the male sex), in a fit of crazed ecumenism Bishop Cahal Daly recently maintained that Unionism and Nationalism were *both* 'noble aspirations'. It would be preferable to downgrade Nationalism to the ignoble status traditionally enjoyed by Unionism, rather than cling to the notion that a 'good' or 'real' Nationalism exists in some zone uncontaminated by the Provos. We could also give 'aspirations' a rest. Fintan O'Toole has argued (*The Irish Times*, 20 April 1989) that Section 31 permits physical-force Republicanism to function as the *id* of the body politic. It subsists at an unconscious level where it cannot be interrogated. And if Sinn Féin remains below interrogation, the SDLP (a political party after all) remains above it. Thus Southern Nationalism cedes control over its own redefinition. The very structure of the New Ireland Forum, in asserting the unity of the Nationalist family, excluded agonising reappraisal of other unitary principles. Nevertheless, *de facto* reappraisal takes place all the time: at the level of economic necessity, historical revisionism, cultural change, the cycles of shock and weariness over the Northern war.

Literature makes a good barometer of asymmetric consciousness in Ireland. As a literary critic who sometimes notices distinctive elements in Northern writing, I have been suspected equally of partisanship and partitionism. This looks like another over-anxious unitary reflex. It is absurd to contend that Northern Ireland and the Republic have had identical socio-political experiences since 1922, or since 1968. And if we believe that literature is (up to a point) conditioned by society, and criticises society, we should not sacrifice any insights it can offer. For instance, I have certainly learned more about the culture of the North from Medbh McGuckian's or Seamus Heaney's poetry (even after his move to Dublin), and that of the Republic from Paul Durcan's or Thomas McCarthy's.

Durcan's visionary radicalism, for instance, criticises a particular *status quo*. Unlike the majority of Southern poets, he broaches the North. But he does so from outside the territory, without inhabiting its tensions as do the imaginations of Muldoon or Heaney. And Durcan's special focus is to open up the Republic's implication in the war. Thus long before Enniskillen he wrote the satirical 'National

Day of Mourning for Twelve Protestants'. Life slowly catches up with art. Durcan's poetry neither renounces its own cultural roots nor overlooks Loyalist terror. But he concentrates on the spiritual failings of the society he knows and for which he feels responsible. So, generally, do other writers North and South. An exception that proves the rule may be recent fiction and drama from the Southern border counties, which contains two-way perspectives from a neglected limbo and source of light. But the Republic's writers are distinctively obsessed with secularism, sexuality, socialism, versions of feminism, and other libertarian themes. Literature and theatre seem to be mounting a communal psycho-drama that releases what the official political culture won't admit.

Field Day is often perceived as speaking for Ireland. The company has indeed sometimes sponsored pluralism: in staging Stewart Parker's *Pentecost*, in publishing a pamphlet by Unionist Robert McCartney. But the pamphlet-topics so far chosen give a Northern Nationalist priority to cultural and political 'decolonisation'. The latest trio was written by foreign literary critics better acquainted with general theories of colonialism than with Ireland after 1922. For Edward Said and Terry Eagleton, all 'the Irish people' are still engaged in a single National struggle. Reviewing the pamphlets (*Fortnight* no 271), Colm Toibin found a time-warp in Field Day's own perceptions: 'the social and cultural revolution of the 1960s has left the artists in the Field Day group singularly unmoved ... They write as though nothing had ever changed: their Ireland is distinctly pre-decimal. Thus England is the problem and the enemy (and the dramatic *other*).' Field Day's latest production *Saint Oscar* looked out of date in Dublin because it was an instance of the re-imported Nationalist propaganda I mentioned earlier. Its author, Eagleton again, used Wilde to present a timeless thesis about imperialist oppression. Field Day's eagerness to collude with the hoary stereotypes of the English hard Left seems significant.

Common to Friel's drama and the critical writings of Seamus Deane is a powerful sense of Palestinian dispossession. The alienation of Friel's Ballybeg is utterly different from the post-Nationalist alienation of Tom Murphy's *Bailegangaire*. When speaking of Ireland's literary and political traditions, Deane repeatedly uses the terms 'crisis' and 'discontinuity'. These conditions he generalises to cover the total past and this total island now. But his perceptions cannot be divorced from the recent history of Derry with its lost hinterland. (The other side of this bleak coin is the siege-haunted Derry Protestant.) The same affiliation may show itself in Deane's intellectual resistance to the 'mystique of Irishness' concocted by Yeats on the one hand, Corkery on the other. Perhaps his otherwise rather extreme (and contradictory) desire for 'new writing, new politics, unblemished by Irishness, but securely Irish' (*Heroic Styles*) reflects, and aspires to redress, the exclusion of Northern Nationalists from the self-images and cultural definitions that became operational in the new state. Certainly, critics associated with Field Day approach the Irish Literary Revival both as a colonial manifestation, and as a present hegemony (not a receding phase in literary history). They question the Revival's cultural power as revisionists question the political power of 1916. As for Corkery, Tom Garvin argues that Munster, remote from *both* Ulster communities, played a disproportionate part in theorising the revolution (see *Nationalist Revolutionaries in Ireland* 1858-1928). Perhaps that explains the tiff between John A Murphy and Nell McCafferty.

Whatever its other purposes and qualities, the Field Day project for 'a comprehensive anthology' of Irish literature ('what writing in this country has been') shows a desire to influence definitions. Within the literary sphere it seeks to piece together a broken past, to go back behind all deforming colonisation, to return to origins (550 AD), and thus to clarify 'Irish reality' so that we can start again. In contrast, revisionism seeks to break down a monolithic idea of the past, to go back behind the revolution's ideology, to return to origins in 1922 and understand them more empirically. In my view the former project risks the dangerous fantasy that loss and breakdown can be retrieved. Rather than start a new literary and political clock, I think we should try to tell the time accurately.

JOHN HUME AND 'AN ISLAND ONCE AGAIN'

Political language goes out of date when its objective basis shrinks. It's easy to see that Sinn Féin inhabits a rhetorical dead-end - though their terminology should be directly challenged in the Republic, *the only place where it can be*. But what about the political language of John Hume? Does he breathe new life into Nationalist ideology? Or (like Field Day at times) does he simply translate traditional concepts into an updated idiom?

Hume keeps his political unconscious under better control than do Haughey, Maginness and O'Fiaich. He thus seems a model of eloquent flexibility as compared with the monotonous negatives of Unionism. But Unionism may be a better critic than author - or at least a close reader of the subtexts that concern it. And on closer inspection Hume's language has much in common with George Orwell's metaphor for Marxist jargon: 'prefabricated phrases bolted together like the pieces of a child's Meccano set'.

Hume likes to stress that he has moved beyond the old definitions. So let us test him on the questions of 'Irishness' and 'Revisionism'. On the former topic he has criticised 'those who are so unsure of their Irishness that they need to remind us of it constantly' (thus acknowledging competition between the SDLP and Sinn Féin over degrees of Irishness). And he has rejected the Republican category of 'the Irish people', favouring instead: 'Protestant fellow Irishmen', 'the people of this island', 'the Unionist people and the rest of the people of this island' (*London Review of Books*, 2 February 1989). But is this quite as innocent and open as it looks? Or is it the 'particular case' which it suits to say that they are Irish? Hume's article does not call the Unionist people 'British', thus minimising the significance of this self-protective definition in their own consciousness. Again, while Ireland as island is an improvement on Ireland as nation, it omits 'the totality of relations in the archipelago'. Although Hume's vision is larger than that of most Northern politicians he too selects the 'whole' on which he desires attention to concentrate. Nobody catches all the snooker-balls in the triangle.

Hume's *cultural* perception of his 'Protestant fellow Irishmen' is remarkably narrow. It excludes most of their affiliations to the other island - and indeed to this one. He characterises their 'long and strong tradition in Ireland' as religious, military, industrial: 'pride in their service to the crown ... in their work ethic and in their faith'. Obviously there is truth here, but limited, stereotypical and dated. Meanwhile 'Irishness', so 'sure' as to be given no definition whatsoever, seems another matter entirely. (It also seems, unlike Unionism, to have no religious affiliation.) Hume's incomplete, and unconsciously polarised, cultural awareness may reflect the binary geography of Derry.

As for Revisionism: Hume contributed an article on 'Europe of the Regions' to Richard Kearney's compilation *Across the Frontiers: Ireland in the* 1990s. The contrast between it and the editor's own contribution illustrates once again the uneven development of Nationalist consciousness. This is the post-Nationalist Kearney:

> An Ireland without frontiers is obviously an Ireland without borders. This does not, however, entail a united Ireland in the traditional sense of the term. For the nation-states of Britain and Ireland, which constitute the very basis for the opposing claims of Nationalist and Unionist ideologies would be superseded by a European constellation of regions.

Hume's Europe, in contrast, becomes less and less regional the closer it gets to home. He does not advocate Ulster regionalism, or any other form of Irish Balkanisation, but emphasises what 1992 will do for the Gaeltacht. And he falls into Nationalist idiom: 'the real "new republicanism" ... rather than being any reversal of the national destiny ... will allow us better to fulfil our potential as a people ... and to enjoy properly the inchoate European outlook and vision which was lost in our oppressive and obsessive relationship with Britain'. Wearing his SDLP hat, Hume remains interested in a relationship which his Euro-regionalist hat occludes.

When interviewed in *The Irish Times* by Frank Millar (13 January 1989), Hume endlessly repeated the unitary Meccano- phrase 'this island', *not* 'these islands': 'the central relationship being that of the Unionists and the rest of this island and *then* the relationship between Ireland and Britain' (my italics); 'Going to the heart of the problem is the relationship between the Unionist people and the rest of the people of this island'; 'do they want [to] work out with the rest of the people of this island how we share the island?' 'What I want to see is the representatives of the divided people of this island reaching an agreement on how they share the island ...'

In a kind of linguistic tug-of-war, Hume first tries to yank the Unionists off their UK base, then to pull them across the border. 'Island-sharing' (I wonder how keen they are in Kerry?) is a very different matter from 'power-sharing' within the existing framework. Hume is in fact skilfully playing a political word and map game with specific origins in Northern Irish politics. There, trying to control bounds and definitions has always been part of the territorial battle. But Unionists are unlikely to swallow his island-Nationalism unless Nationalism equally swallows their archipelagan-Britishness. Britain and the Republic find themselves guarantors of communities more Unionist and more Nationalist than themselves, for whose neurotic pathologies their own incoherence is much to blame. Only by rethinking their own relationship, outside existing Nationalist and Unionist categories, can Ireland and Britain generate new political language for their frontier-region.

WOMEN AND NATIONALISM

I have compared Irish Nationalism to bad poetry. In bad poems the relations between word, image and life break down. Political images, like political language (from which they are never quite distinct), eventually exhaust themselves or prove incapable of renewal. I think this happens at the juncture where the image Women-Ireland-Muse meets contemporary Irish women. There, I believe, the breakdown of Nationalist ideology becomes particularly clear.

In the film *Mother Ireland* (Derry Film and Video) Nell McCafferty regrets that the Committee for the Liberation of Irish Women, to avert a potential split, decided not to talk about the North. She would now welcome general debate on topics like 'Feminism and Physical Force'. While I might hope for a different outcome than she does, I agree that the issue of women and Nationalism cannot be dodged for ever. Southern women too are implicated in this issue, although they may neither know it nor wish it. Even on her death-bed Cathleen-Anorexia exerts a residual power over the image and self-images of *all* Irish women. Both at home and abroad, she still confers status on selected kinds of Irish womanness (not, for instance, the Rhonda Paisley kind). The absurd 'Irish' edition of *Spare Rib* (August 1989), of which more anon, is a case in point.

Of course the Ulster Protestant community, though dragged forward faster by Westminster legislation, is as traditionally patriarchal as Catholic Nationalism. This tribe too has its cult of male chieftains: Carson, Moses, the Big Man (compare Dev, the Pope, the Boss). And the whole country abounds in Ancient Orders of Hibernian Male-Bonding: lodges, brotherhoods, priesthoods, hierarchies, sodalities, knights, Fitzwilliam Tennis Club, Field Day Theatre Company. But at least Unionism does not appropriate the image of woman or hide its aggressions behind our skirts. Nor does it - as a reactive ideology - seek ideological mergers. A Unionist feminist might be these things separately, though genuine Feminism would erode her Unionism. A Nationalist/Republican feminist, less readily regarded as a contradiction in terms, claims that her ideologies coincide. And in so doing she tries to hijack Irish Feminism.

Terry Eagleton (in *Nationalism: Irony and Commitment*) develops an analogy between Nationalism and Feminism as responses to 'oppression'. He argues that Nationalism must not prematurely sell its soul to revisionism and pluralism, just as Feminism - until women have been truly liberated - must not sell its soul to 'a troubling and subverting of all sexual strait-jacketing'. As I will indicate later, with respect to the history of women and Nationalism, strait-jackets tend to remain in place after the revolution unless their removal has been intrinsic to the revolution. Eagleton does not recognise that Catholic Nationalism has often been as great an oppressor of Irish people, Irish women, as British imperialism or Ulster Unionism. Perhaps the equivalent of advanced feminist 'troubling and subverting' is precisely what our Nationalist and Unionist patriarchal strait-jackets need.

Subversions occur wherever Protestants and Catholics in Ulster evade the binary ideological trap. But we need help from the Republic. I was surprised that Eavan Boland's LIP pamphlet, *A Kind of Scar: The Woman Poet in a National Tradition*, ignored the extent to which the North has destabilised the 'nation'. Boland holds to unitary assumptions about 'a society, a nation, a literary heritage'. Troubled about 'the woman poet', she takes the 'national tradition' for granted - and perhaps thereby misses a source of her trouble. Because *A Kind of Scar* activates only one pole of its dialectic, it does not evolve the radical aesthetic it promises. By not asking *why* 'as a poet I could not easily do without the idea of a nation', Boland fails to challenge an idea of Irish poetry which is narrow as well as patriarchal. She refers to 'marginality *within* a tradition' (my italics) and regrets that 'the Irish nation as an existing construct in Irish poetry was not available to me', without considering how that construct itself, both inside and outside poetry, has marginalised and scarred many Irish women and men.

Earlier I suggested that to over-stress the independence of Irish literature from English literature (and *vice versa*) distorts literary history and does not help contemporary politics. Boland, it seems to me, feels unnecessarily guilty for (as an apprentice poet) having read 'English court poetry' on Achill, and having imitated the English 'Movement' mode of the early sixties. To whom, to what avatar, to what icon is she apologising?

In fact, it is to Mother Ireland herself. Although Boland criticises male poets for having made woman a silent object in their visionary odes (to 'Dark Rosaleen. Cathleen Ni Houlihan. The nation as woman: the woman as national muse'), she insists: 'in all this I did not blame nationalism'. Because she does not blame Nationalism, her alternative Muse turns out to be the twin sister of Dark Rosaleen etc: 'the truths of womanhood and the defeats of a nation. An improbable intersection?' No, as Conor Cruise O'Brien said in a similar context, 'a dangerous intersection'. Boland's new Muse, supposedly based on the varied historical experience of Irish women, looks remarkably like the Sean Bhean Bhocht. Her pamphlet begins by invoking an old Achill woman who speaks of the Famine. The 'real women of an actual past' are subsumed into a single emblematic victim-figure: 'the women of a long struggle and a terrible survival', 'the wrath and grief of Irish history'. By not questioning the nation, Boland recycles the literary cliche from which she desires to escape.

Boland notes that 'the later Yeats' is a rare exception among poets who 'have feminised the national and nationalised the feminine'. There are good reasons why this should be so. Yeats's early play *Cathleen Ni Houlihan* helped to propagate the feminine mystique of Irish Nationalism. During the three years after 1916, in such poems as 'On a Political Prisoner' and the much-misunderstood 'A Prayer for my Daughter', he broke the icon his poetry had gilded. That is, he questioned Cathleen as then incarnated by Constance Markievicz and Maud Gonne MacBride.

In 'A Prayer for my Daughter' Yeats criticises Ireland/Gonne for her 'opinionated mind'. By 'opinion' he always means dogmatic nationalism. So he is revising his image of Woman-Ireland-Muse, and divining Anorexia in Gonne 'choked with hate':

> Have I not seen the loveliest woman born
> Out of the mouth of plenty's horn
> Because of her opinionated mind
> Barter that horn and every good
> By quiet natures understood
> For an old bellows full of angry wind?

That 'old bellows' is already full of destructive cliches. Yeats may be patriarchal in the female qualities he values above ideological rigidity: 'natural kindness', 'heart-revealing intimacy', 'courtesy', rootedness'. But it might be argued that at least he replaces the aisling of Nationalist male fantasy with a model for the Irish future that draws on (some of) women's own qualities - the 'womanly times' for which Ian McEwan has called.

However, Gonne, Markievicz and Maeve the warrior-queen have enjoyed a new lease of life in Northern Republican ideology. Perhaps Feminists too readily assume that it's *always* a good thing when passive versions of women are transformed into active ones. Both have political uses.

Two passive images are the vulnerable virgin and the mourning mother: images that link Cathleen with Mary. They project the self-image of Catholic Nationalism as innocent victim, equally oppressed at all historical periods. (Is there a subconscious admission that Irish men victimise women?) This assigns to Britain the perpetual role of male bully and rapist. In Seamus Heaney's 'Ocean's Love to Ireland': 'The ruined maid complains in Irish'. In the mid-1970s Heaney could still symbolise the Northern conflict as 'a struggle between the cults and devotees of a god and a goddess'; between 'an indigenous territorial numen, a tutelar of the whole island, call her Mother Ireland, Kathleen Ni Houlihan ... the Shan Van Vocht, whatever' and 'a new male cult whose founding fathers were Cromwell, William of Orange and Edward Carson'. To characterise Irish Nationalism (only constructed in the nineteenth century) as archetypally female both gives it mythic pedigree and exonerates it from aggressive and oppressive intent. Its patriarchal elements also disappear. Here, perhaps, we glimpse the *poetic* unconscious of Northern Nationalism. At the same time, Heaney's mouldering 'Bog Queen' in *North* may indirectly represent the cult of Cathleen as a death-cult. The book contains an unresolved tension between two Muses: a symbolic mummified or mummifying woman (not yet Anorexia) and the warmly creative, life-giving aunt who bakes scones in the poem 'Sunlight'.

While Virgin-Ireland gets raped and pitied, Mother Ireland translates pity into a call to arms and vengeance. She resembles the white-feather-bestowing 'Little Mother' in First-World-War recruiting. Traditionally, it is her *sons* whom Mother Ireland recruits and whose *manhood* she tests. More recently, some of her daughters have also become 'freedom-fighters'. In *Mother Ireland* Bernadette Devlin and Mairead Farrell differed in their attitudes to the personification. Devlin felt that Mother Ireland had empowered her as a strong woman; Farrell said: 'Mother Ireland, get off our backs'. But did she? Is there not collusion between all feminine-Nationalist images, between Queen Maeve and Mother Ireland, between the feminine-pathetic and the feminine-heroic? The latter too disguises or softens aggression: the looks and dress of Gonne and Markievicz were propaganda-assets. On the cover of the biased *Only The Rivers Run Free: Northern Ireland: The Women's War* a glamorous young paramilitary woman fronts a desperate-looking Sean Bhean.

Such images of Irish women are among those selectively approved by Anorexia. The cover of *Spare Rib* (August 1989) features another: a West Belfast Mother Courage with child in pram, smoke and flames behind her, and insets of a British soldier and 'Stop Strip Searches'. Of course there are many courageous working-class mothers on the Falls - ditto on the Shankill. But does it help them if this magazine distorts the profile of Irish women to include no police or UDR widows; no non-aligned social-workers, doctors or teachers; no members of the DUP; no Belfast or Dublin yuppies; no Southern feminists; no TDs? There are also articles with titles like 'Britain's War on Ireland' and 'Irish in Britain - Living in the Belly of the Beast' (an interesting variation on rape-images: cannibalism? Jonah and the whale?). And a literary section, among other poetic sentimentalities, reprints Susan Langstaff Mitchell's 'To the Daughters of Erin': 'Rise from your knees, O daughters rise! / Our mother still is young and fair ... Heroes shall leap from every hill ... The red blood burns in Ireland still'. (Feminism, where are you?) *Spare Rib* has certainly provided the most ludicrous instance yet of the British Left's anachronistic and self-righteous pieties on Ireland. But it's up to Irish women themselves to expose the loaded terms in a statement like: 'In the *Six Counties Irish* women experience *oppression* both as women and as members of a *colonised people*' (my italics). I attended a *Time To Go* conference in London which offered a seminar on 'Ireland in Feminism'. I think Feminism in Ireland should have something to say about that.

During the Irish revolution Nationalist women discovered - though not all acknowledged or cared - that their oppression as women did not end with the Dawning of the Day. The briefly eulogised 'Dáil Girl ... wielding a cudgel in one hand and a revolver in the other' soon gave way to Dev's ideal of 'life within the home'. Nor had the Dáil girl necessarily taken up her cudgel for Feminism.

As a general rule: the more Republican, the less Feminist. The ultra-Nationalism of the six women deputies who opposed the Treaty was, in Margaret Ward's words, governed by the 'ghosts of dead sons, husbands and brothers'. Theirs were 'opinionated minds' with no - female? - capacity for compromise, and they set a pattern for the limited participation of women in the Free State/Republic's political life: almost invariably licensed by male relatives, by dynastic privilege. Rosemary Cullen Owens in *Smashing Times* (less romantic than Ward's *Unmanageable Revolutionaries*) brings out the tension between Nationalism and Suffragism: 'From 1914 onwards, with Home Rule on the statute book, it was the growing separatist movement which created the greatest obstacle to a united women's movement'.

Sinn Féin women (the only women quoted in *Spare Rib*) have recently adopted some Feminist ideas. But they cling, like their elder sisters, to the prospective goodwill of Republican men, and to the fallacy that: 'there can't be women's liberation until there's national liberation'. Devlin in *Spare Rib* seems significantly wary of 'the gospel according to the Holy Writ of Feminism'. What a woman 'needs to know is that we, her sisters, will catch her if she stumbles, help her find the questions - the answers she must find herself'. Who are 'we, her sisters'? And what kind of elitism lurks in Devlin's assertion (in *Mother Ireland*) that 'the best young feminist women today are those who have come through the experience of the Republican movement'?

While admiring the bonding that tough circumstances beget, and perceiving these circumstances as tragic, I do not accept that either the supportiveness of the ghetto or the essential survival-strategy in Armagh Gaol affords a model for Irish women in general. The basis of such bonding is tribal rather than sisterly. It remains true that the vast majority of Republican women come from traditionally Republican families - recruited by and for a patriarchal unit. The Irish Women's Movement, instead of walking away or vaguely empathising, might examine the role of Nationalist conditioning in all this: the ideological forces which played a part in sending out Mairead Farrell to be shot.

Contrary to Nell McCafferty, I think that 'Feminism and Physical Force' is self-evidently a contradiction in terms. Years ago a member of the Irish Women's Franchise League said: 'It is our conviction feminism and militarism are natural born enemies and cannot flourish in the same soil'. Militarism, that touch of Madame Defarge, gives the Sinn Féin sisterhood its faintly chilling aura. In *The Demon Lover: On the Sexuality of Terrorism*, Robin Morgan argues that revolutionary terrorism inevitably involves a death-cult. It enacts the quest of the male hero who already 'lives as a dead man'. She asks: 'Why is manhood always perceived as the too-high price of peace?' and notes that when men take over any movement: 'what once aimed for a humanistic triumph now aims for a purist defeat. Martyrdom'. The same syndrome can be detected in Protestant anticipations of Armageddon, apocalypse, their last stand (the ghosts of religious wars walk on both sides). Morgan's conclusion mirrors the Irish Nationalist historical pattern: 'The rebel woman in a male-defined State-that-would-be is merely acting out another version of the party woman running for office in the State-that-is'. Unionist party-women have been equally acquiescent in militarism.

Cathleen-Anorexia encourages women to join a male death- cult which has a particularly masochistic martyrology. This cult's rituals deny the 'connectivity' which Morgan sees as the 'genius' of feminist thought: 'In its rejection of the static, this capacity is witty and protean, like the dance of nature itself ... It is therefore a volatile capacity - dangerous to every imaginable status quo, because of its insistence on *noticing*. Such a noticing involves both attentiveness and recognition, and is in fact a philosophical and activist technique for being in the world, as well as for changing the world'. In 'Easter 1916' Yeats understands that 'Too long a sacrifice / Can make a stone of the heart', and contrasts that stone with 'the living stream'. Surely the chill, the stone, the self-destructiveness at the heart of Irish Nationalism shows up in its abuse of women and their gifts of life.

CONCLUSION: AFTER ANOREXIA

I have argued that Nationalism and Unionism in Ireland are dying ideologies, death-cult ideologies. Yet these ideologies are also masks for an intensely local territorial struggle. Ulster's territorial imperative has produced a politics which pivots on male refusal to give an inch. John Hewitt characterises the Protestant people as 'stubborn'; Seamus Heaney characterises the Catholic people as 'obstinate'.

But this polarised *macho* politics travesties the North's cultural complexity. In the report on *Cultural Traditions in Northern Ireland* Brian Turner emphasises how the thriving local studies movement has 'challenged the "two traditions" terminology'. And Anthony Buckley in 'Collecting Ulster's Culture: Are There Really Two Traditions?', illustrates ways in which culture has been caricatured for the purpose of 'asserting group identities'. A more negative term for this is 'cultural defence'. In fact insecurities underlie the self-assertive rhetorics of both Unionism and Nationalism. Cultural defence is the reflex of frontier-regions where communities fear extinction or absorption. It explains, for instance, the Catholic Church's not-an-inch attitude to integrated education. And it explains

Unionism's perennial paranoia about the Irish language (only now to be properly supported and thus depoliticised).

That the Free State's Gaelicisation policy attracted more Unionist jeers than did Rome Rule indicates fears of ethnic exclusion (and also the counter-productiveness of Nationalist ideology). Yet Gaelicisation, which attempted an *impossible* separation of Irishness from Britishness, was itself a form of cultural defence. Its errors are reproduced today by Sinn Féin's cultural self-ghettoisation. There is a sad element of barren triumphalism in the West Belfast Festival.

Locked into dying ideologies, a territorial imperative and cultural defence, Northern Irish people do not immediately hold all the keys to their own salvation. One key is held by the Republic and Britain; another by a slow process of education.

Firstly, only the Republic and Britain together can defuse the mutual fear of their client communities. This should involve the Republic honestly re-examining its own Nationalism; making its constitutional claim as inoperative in theory as it is in practice; and adopting the same hands-off stance as the UK government. (John Hume's argument that the British have thereby left matters up to the people of Ireland should be resisted.) Advance depends on an intricately engineered four-wheel drive which engages all parties to the dispute, and which encourages momentum within the North.

Secondly, without education in the broadest sense we cannot loosen the grip of Anorexia, of ideological *rigor mortis*. Progress will not only stem from official or institutional sources - Education for Mutual Understanding, Co-operation North, putting Cultural Traditions on the curriculum etc - it occurs wherever people work together practically and constructively. Yet, as with the Irish language, we also need more formal means to dismantle the frameworks of cultural defence.

One pilot-model is the local studies movement. This, at the micro-level, breaks down monolithic versions of Nationalist and Unionist history. It also maximises the strength rather than the weakness of Ulster's territorial imperative: attachment to place. Local studies promote the 'noticing' that Robin Morgan values. Many Unionists (the OUP wing) refuse to notice the ground under their own feet, the very territory they claim. Since 1922 they have often imported an anxious, ersatz and self-mutilating Englishness to stand in for Britishness and fend off Irishness. The Campaign for Equal Citizenship (for getting British parties to organise in Northern Ireland) is a recent instance of Unionists staring across the water and trying to walk on it. Really, they are motivated by political sulks and cultural defence in the wake of Agreement. Unionist attempts to base themselves in London, like the SDLP inclination to identify with Dublin, show the vital importance of the Regionalist concept. Some local councils now lead the way in power-sharing, as local studies do in culture-sharing.

Another model - which gives the lie to equations of the Regional with the provincial - is Northern writing, especially since the early 1960s. At the start of this pamphlet I called literature the primary place where language changes and anorexic categories are exposed (not always a conscious process). Writers born into an over-determined, over-defined environment, into a tension between political simplicities and cultural complexity, have felt impelled to redefine: to explore and criticise language, images, categories, stereotypes, myths. Northern writing does not fit the binary shapes cut out by Nationalism and Unionism. It trellises the harsh girders with a myriad details. It overspills borders and manifests a web of affiliation that stretches beyond any heartland - to the rest of Ireland, Britain, Europe. But the range of styles, histories, myths and influences perhaps could only enter the imagination in this unique zone of 'problems and cleavages' (John Hewitt's phrase). All the 'cultural traditions' count somewhere; nor are the political divisions discounted.

There is a third model in women's groups whose generally pragmatic priorities have theoretical implications. These groups exemplify how we learn and teach by doing. Recently, when the sectarianism of that male-dominated mayhem, Belfast City Council, blocked a grant to the Falls Road Women's Centre, their indignation was shared by the Women's Centre on the Shankill.

The image of the web is female, feminist, 'connective' - as contrasted with male polarisation. So is the ability to inhabit a range of relations rather than a single allegiance. The term 'identity' has been coarsened in Ulster politics to signify two ideological package-deals immemorially on offer. To admit to more varied, mixed, fluid and relational kinds of identity would advance nobody's territorial claim. It would undermine cultural defences. It would subvert the male pride that keeps up the double frontier-siege. All this would be on the side of life - like noticing, redefining and again redefining, doing.

Bernard Crick argues:

> While nationalisms are real and authentic in these islands, yet none are as self-sufficient as their adepts claim. In Northern Ireland most people are, in fact, torn in two directions: 'torn', that is, while their political leaders will not recognise that people can, with dignity, face in two directions culturally at once, and refuse to invent political institutions to match. In the world before nation-states such dualities and pluralities were common enough, as in some other border-areas today.
> *Irish Review*, 5, Autumn 1988

Both Irish Nationalism and Ulster Unionism must accept the reality of the North as a frontier-region, a cultural corridor, a zone where Ireland and Britain permeate one another. The Republic should cease to talk about 'accommodating diversity' and face up to duality. This would actually help the North to relax into a less dualistic sense of its own identity: to function, under whatever administrative format, as a shared region of these islands. At which point there will definitely be no such person as Cathleen Ni Houlihan.

REFERENCES AND FURTHER READING

Boland, Eavan. *A Kind of Scar: The Woman Poet In A National Tradition* Dublin: Attic Press (LIP Pamphlet), 1989

Buckley, Anthony. In *The Use of Tradition* Alan Gailey (ed) Cultra: Ulster Folk and Transport Museum, 1988

Dawe, Gerald and Edna Longley (eds). *Across a Roaring Hill: The Protestant Imnagination in Modern Ireland* Belfast: Blackstaff, 1985

Eagleton, Terry. *Nationalism: Irony and Commitment* Derry: Field Day Pamphlet No 13, 1988

Foster, Roy. *Modern Ireland 1600-1972* London: Allen Lane: The Penguin Press, 1988

Garvin, Tom. *Nationalist Revolutionaries in Ireland 1858-1928* Oxford: Clarendon Press, 1987

Kearney, Richard. *Across the Frontiers: Ireland in the 1990s* Dublin: Wolfhound Press, 1989

Morgan, Robin. *The Demon Lover: On the Sexuality of Terrorism* London: Methuen, 1989

O'Halloran, Clare. *Partition and the Limits of Irish Nationalism: An Ideology Under Stress* Dublin: Gill and MacMillan, 1987

Owens, Rosemary Cullen. *Smashing Times: A History of the Irish Women's Suffrage Movement 1889-1992* Dublin: Attic Press, 1984

Said, Edward. *Yeats and Decolonisation* Derry: Field Day Pamphlet No 15, 1988

Turner, Brian. Local Studies Section in *Cultural Traditions in Northern Ireland* Belfast: Queen's University Institute of Irish Studies, 1989

Ward, Margaret. *Unmanageable Revolutionaries* Dingle: Brandon Press / London: Pluto Press, 1983